63/5

A New True Book

NUTRITION

By Leslie Jean LeMaster

This "true book" was prepared under the direction of
William H. Wehrmacher, M.D., FACC, FACP
Clinical Professor of Medicine and
Adjunct Professor of Physiology
Loyola University Stritch School of Medicine
with the help of his granddaughter Cheryl Sabey

Φ
CHILDREN'S PRESS
A Division of Grolier Publishing
Sherman Turnpike
Danbury, Connecticut 06816

SCHOOL

ADRIAN, MI 49221

PHOTO CREDITS

EKM-Nepenthe:
© Peter Tartsanyi—2
© Jeffrey Thomas—19 (right fourth), 43

Nawrocki Stock Photo:
© Carlos Vergara—4 (bottom left)
© Jerry Howard—4 (bottom right), 44 (bottom right)
© Jim Whitmer—4 (top right), 24
© W.S. Nawrocki—8 (left), 19 (top, bottom second), 29 (left), 30 (bottom second, bottom fourth)
© Jerry Saxon—10, 44 (top right)
© Jeffrey Apoian—19 (bottom first)
© Larry Brooks—21
© Candee—29 (right)
© Ken Sexton—Cover, 32 (top)
© Donner—39

Cameramann International Ltd.—4 (top left), 26, 27 (bottom left), 32 (bottom left, bottom right), 37 (2 photos)

Tom Stack & Associations:
© Eldon L. Reeves—7 (right)
© Tom Stack—17, 27 (bottom right), 44 (top left), 45

Jerry Hennen—7 (left)

Hillstrom Stock Photo:
© Bill Barksdale—8 (right)
© Art Brown—15 (right), 23, 27 (top), 44 (bottom left)
© Don and Pat Valenti—31 (bottom right)
© Richard L. Capps—28
© Ray Hillstrom—31 (top right)
© Charlene Faris—38

Journalism Services:
© Steve Sumner—12

Art Pahlke—15 (left)

Stock Imagery:
© Cornelius Hogenbirk—19 (right second, third, fifth), 30 (left), 31 (top left)
© B. Payne—30 (bottom third)
© R. Ellian—31 (bottom middle)
© Orion—35

Image Finders:
© Bob Skelly—19 (bottom third, fourth), 31 (bottom left)

Marilyn Gartman Agency:
© Lee Balterman—40

Library of Congress Cataloging in Publication Data

LeMaster, Leslie Jean.
  Nutrition.

  (A New true book)
  Includes index
  Summary: A simple explanation of our bodies'
nutritional needs, specifically discussing vitamins,
minerals, proteins, fats, carbohydrates, and water,
as well as the diseases caused by a lack of these
nutrients.
  1. Nutrition—Juvenile literature. 2. Malnutrition—
Juvenile literature. [1. Nutrition. 2. Malnutrition]
I. Title.
QP141.L435   1985   613.2   85-7728
ISBN 0-516-01271-1   AACR2

TABLE OF CONTENTS

Your cells need energy to do
their work. Your body uses the food you
eat to feed these cells.

WHY IS EATING IMPORTANT?

Almost everyone will agree that eating is fun. Food tastes good, especially when you are hungry and you like the food you are eating. But you are really eating to feed your body's cells so that they have the energy to do their work.

WHAT IS NUTRITION?

Nutrition is the process by which plants and animals take in and use food. The materials in food that the body can use are called nutrients. Nutrients are divided into six groups: proteins, fats, carbohydrates, water, vitamins, and minerals.

When nutrients are digested, they are broken down into simpler materials so that they can be passed through body membranes, absorbed into the blood, and carried to body cells.

Plants get their nutrients from the soil and air. They grow with the help of energy from the sun.

Plants, such as sunflowers (left) and lettuce (right), get food from the soil and air. They get energy from the sun.

Animals, such as the orangutan (left) and dairy cattle (right), get the nutrients they need from the food they eat.

Animals and people need a certain amount of nutrients every day so that their cells can do their work properly. A balanced diet of different foods will give them all the nourishment they need in order to grow strong and healthy.

WHAT ARE PROTEINS?

Proteins are composed of twenty amino acids, or building blocks, that are linked together in different combinations.

The body can produce more than half of its amino acids from ordinary foods. But the others, called "essential amino acids," must come from certain special foods.

Different proteins serve different functions. They form parts of the structures of muscle, hair, skin, nails, connective tissue, and glands.

The main function of protein is to build the working body tissues.

Runners use up great amounts of energy during each race.

WHAT ARE FATS?

Fats supply the body with energy. They are one of the main sources of calories. A calorie is the unit that is used to measure energy. If the body takes in more fats (or calories) than it can burn up in activity, then the body stores the extra energy as fat. If too much

It is best to lose weight when you are young. Scientists
have discovered that children of overweight parents are
more than likely to be overweight than children of normal
weight parents.

fat is stored in the body, a
person becomes overweight.
Being overweight, like
being underweight, is
bad for health.

WHAT ARE CARBOHYDRATES?

Carbohydrates are composed of starches and sugars. When eaten, carbohydrates can combine with oxygen and release energy for the body to do its work. Carbohydrates that are not used up in energy are stored in the body and changed into fat.

HOW IS WATER USED AS A NUTRIENT?

Water is an essential nutrient. Two thirds of the entire body is composed of water. Water is necessary for blood circulation, carrying nutrients to cells, getting rid of wastes, and controlling body

People need water in order to live.

temperature. Water you lose through normal body processes must be replaced with water from foods and drinks.

WHAT ARE VITAMINS?

Vitamins are nutrients that the body needs to stay alive and healthy. Vitamins are contained in special foods.

Each vitamin does a certain job in the body. But no vitamin can do the job of any other vitamin. So it is important to eat a good diet of many different

kinds of foods. That way, the body can get all the vitamins it needs.

When scientists first discovered that the body needs vitamins, they named each vitamin after a letter of the alphabet, A through K. Now some vitamins are called by their chemical names and others keep their letter names.

Vitamin B was found to be not just one vitamin, but many separate vitamins. Altogether, all the B vitamins are called the vitamin B complex.

We need vitamins to stay alive, but only in tiny amounts. Taking large doses of some vitamins, like vitamins A and D, can make us sick.

VITAMIN CHART

VITAMIN	NEEDED FOR	FOOD SOURCES
A (retinol)	The eyes, especially for seeing at night; healthy bones, teeth, and skin; growth of new cells	Milk, butter, and other dairy foods; liver, eggs, carrots, green and yellow vegetables
B_1 (thiamine)	Good appetite; proper function of heart, nervous system, and skin	Pork, liver, yeast, whole-grain bread and cereal, peas, beans, most vegetables
B_2 (riboflavin)	Healthy eyes and skin, especially skin at the edge of the nose and mouth	Milk, poultry, eggs, lean meat, kidney, liver, green and yellow vegetables, enriched bread
Niacin (part of vitamin B complex)	Prevents serious diseases of the skin, digestive system, and nervous system	Liver, lean meat, whole grains, poultry, fish, milk, peas, beans, eggs, yeast, nuts
B_6 (pyridoxine)	Helps the body to use proteins and some fats and to make antibodies to fight disease	Lean meat, whole grains, liver, kidney, fish
Pantothenic acid	Helps the blood change carbohydrates, fats, and proteins into energy	Egg yolks, meat, nuts, whole-grain cereals
B_{12} (cyanocobalamin)	Building red blood cells; proper function of nervous system	Eggs, milk, lean meat, kidney, liver
Biotin	Healthy skin and blood system	Egg yolks, nuts, liver, kidney, most fresh vegetables
Folic acid	Building red blood cells; growth of other cells and tissues; proper function of intestines	Green vegetables, meat, poultry, fish, liver, kidney, whole grains
C (ascorbic acid)	Healthy bones, teeth, and blood vessels; proper function of adrenal glands	Citrus fruits and juices, berries, leafy green vegetables, peppers
D	Bone growth	Fish, eggs, fortified milk and other fortified foods
E (tocopherol)	Red blood cells; protects vitamin A from being destroyed in the body	Whole-grain cereals, lettuce, vegetable oils
K	Blood clotting	Leafy vegetables

WHAT ARE MINERALS?

Minerals are natural substances from the earth's crust. At least fourteen different minerals are necessary for human life. A balanced diet usually gives us all the minerals we need.

The body uses minerals in several ways. Some minerals, like calcium and phosphorus, build teeth and bones. Phosphorus

Some minerals
build teeth.

also helps build nerve and
brain tissue. Iron builds red
blood cells.

Some minerals control
the activities of cells and
organs. Calcium is needed
for muscles to function
properly. Because the heart
is a muscle, calcium is
necessary for the heartbeat.

21

The liquid in blood vessels must have sodium and potassium so that the body's tissues and cells can work properly.

Tiny amounts of other minerals, called trace elements, are also needed. The trace elements include cobalt, copper, magnesium, manganese, zinc, and iodine.

The body needs such small amounts of these minerals that it was once

Minerals keep our bodies strong.

almost impossible for
scientists to measure how
much of them we need.
　But life cannot go on
without these little traces
of special minerals.

WHAT ARE
FOOD GROUPS?

You have learned in this book that you must eat a balanced diet to have a healthy body. This means that you have to eat the kinds of foods that give

your body all the different nutrients it needs.

Food scientists have found that certain kinds of foods contain similar nutrients. These foods are divided into four groups. If you eat foods from each of these food groups every day, your body will get the right amounts of all the important nutrients it needs.

Other foods, such as small amounts of fats and sweets, give the body

Cookies can give you extra energy, but they are not rich in nutrients.

extra calories for more energy.

Here are some examples of foods in the four food groups.

Milk Group: Milk and milk products, cheese, and ice cream. These provide vitamin B_2, vitamin A, protein, calcium, phosphorus, and other nutrients.

The milk group foods include cheese (below left) and milk (below right).

Meat group

Meat Group: Meats, fish, poultry, eggs, dried beans and peas, and nuts. These foods provide vitamin B_1, vitamin B_2, protein, fat, iron, niacin, vitamin B_{12}, and phosphorus.

Bread and cereals group

Bread and Cereals Group: Enriched breads, cereals, spaghetti, macaroni, noodles, and rice. Foods in this group provide vitamin B_1, vitamin B_2, protein, niacin, and iron.

Vegetable and Fruit Group:

1. Dark green leafy and yellow vegetables, like broccoli, asparagus, carrots, green peppers, spinach, turnips, and yellow squash. These provide vitamin A and iron.

Vegetable group

Fruit group

2. Citrus fruits, such as oranges and grapefruit, and also pineapple, strawberries, tomatoes, cantaloupe, and papaya. These provide vitamin C.

Fresh fruits and vegetables are important parts of a balanced diet.

3. Other vegetables and
   fruits: beets, cauliflower,
   celery, corn, lettuce,
   beans, peas, onions, and
   potatoes. Apples,
   bananas, berries,
   cherries, grapes,
   peaches, pears, plums,
   prunes, and watermelon.
   These foods provide
vitamin B_1, vitamin B_2,
calcium, folic acid, iron,
and other nutrients.

WHAT ARE DEFICIENCY DISEASES?

Deficiency diseases are illnesses caused when the body does not get the nutrients it needs for a long period of time. The lack of just one nutrient can make the body very sick.

Protein deficiency is caused by the lack of protein in the diet. It usually develops in babies

These children are healthy and happy.
They have eaten a balanced diet and
have not been deprived of important nutrients.

and children whose diets
consist mainly of sugar,
corn, and starches.

Calorie deficiency is
caused by eating less food
than the body needs. It
may also occur when

some other illness must be cured before the calorie deficiency can be treated.

Symptoms of calorie deficiency include loss of weight, lack of appetite, tiredness, and thinness. In children, calorie deficiency slows down growth.

Calorie deficiency makes most diseases worse, and may make it impossible for the body to fight an infection.

Potatoes (left) and grapefruit (right) are good sources of vitamin C.

Rickets is a deficiency disease caused by lack of vitamin D. Rickets keeps the body from using the calcium in food. This causes the bones to become soft. Soft bones may grow deformed and may bend easily.

Scurvy is caused by a lack of vitamin C. Small blood vessels break easily, causing frequent bruising and swollen gums that bleed easily. It is most commonly found in babies who are not fed fruits, juices, or vegetables.

Vitamin A deficiency causes "night blindness."

This means that the eyes
cannot see in the dark
after being exposed to
bright light. This deficiency
also makes it impossible
for the eyes to see
different shades of gray. It
may also cause eyes to be
unusually dry.

Good nutrition is important no matter how young or old you are.

Pellagra results from lack of niacin and vitamin B_2 in the diet. It usually occurs in people whose diets consist mainly of corn. Symptoms of pellagra include thick, rough blisters on the hands, feet, and face and a sore mouth and tongue.

Beriberi develops from lack of vitamin B_1 and vitamin B_2. It is found among people who live mainly on white rice. Beriberi affects nerves in the legs and arms. It keeps the muscles from moving properly, and causes a buildup of some body fluids, increased heart size, and heart failure.

Iron deficiency anemia is most commonly found in children, in pregnant women, and in people who have lost a lot of blood. Iron deficiency affects blood cells so that they carry less oxygen to other cells in the body.

Salt deficiency is caused when too much salt is lost from the body. Salt and water are lost from heavy sweating in hot weather or

Examples of well-balanced, warm-weather meals

during increased physical activity. Salt deficiency can also result from diarrhea and vomiting. This deficiency causes weakness, stomach cramps, and faintness.

43

Unlike the panda (below left), which needs bamboo leaves in order to survive, humans and many other animals have learned to eat a wide variety of foods.

To end this chapter on a positive side, you should know that many severe deficiency diseases are no longer common in developed countries. So many different foods are available to us that our nutritional needs can be met quite easily.

Here's to good nutrition!

WORDS YOU SHOULD KNOW

amino acids (uh • MEE • no AS • uds) — what proteins are made of

anemia (uh • NEE • mee • uh) — a lack of blood or a lack of red blood cells in the blood

beriberi (bair • ee • BAIR • ee) — a deficiency disease caused by lack of vitamins B_1 and B_2

calorie (KAL • uh • ree) — the basic unit of measuring heat or energy that is supplied to the body by fats

carbohydrates (kar • boh • HI • drates) — compounds of starches and sugars that combine with oxygen to release energy

deficiency disease (dih • FISH • un • see diz • EEZ) — an illness caused by a lack of basic nutrients

fats (FATS) — compounds in certain foods that supply energy to the body

food groups (FOOD GROOPS) — the basic divisions of foods necessary to obtain all the nutrients a body needs

minerals (MIN • uh • rulls) — chemical elements or compounds that occur naturally, at least fourteen of which are needed for a balanced diet

nourishment (NER • ish • munt) — foods and the nutrients they are composed of

nutrients (NOO • tree • unts) — the materials in food that are used by the body to make it healthy

nutrition (noo • TRISH • un) — the process by which a plant or animal takes in food and uses it

pellagra (puh • LAY • gruh) — a deficiency disease caused by lack of niacin and vitamin B_2

proteins (PROH • teens) — combinations of amino acids that contain the elements the body needs to function

rickets (RIK • ets) — a deficiency disease caused by lack of vitamin D

scurvy (SKUR • vee) — a deficiency disease caused by lack of vitamin C

symptoms (SIMP • tuhms) — signs of something being wrong with the body

trace elements (TRAISS EL • uh • munts) — basic minerals needed by the body in trace (very small) amounts

vitamins (VITE • uh • muns) — nutrients contained in special foods and needed by the body to be healthy

INDEX

About the Author

Leslie Jean LeMaster received a Bachelor of Arts Degree in Psychology and has taken postgraduate courses in Clinical and Physiological Psychology. She has written several other books in the New True Book Series, including Your Heart and Blood; Your Brain and Nervous System; Bacteria and Viruses; *and* Cells and Tissues, *all published by Childrens Press. She currently owns and operates her own business in Irvine, California, and is the mother of a ten-year-old daughter.*